WHALES

SPERM WHALES

JOHN F. PREVOST
ABDO & Daughters

Published by Abdo & Daughters, 4940 Viking Drive, Suite 622, Edina, Minnesota 55435.

Library bound edition distributed by Rockbottom Books, Pentagon Tower, P.O. Box 36036, Minneapolis, Minnesota 55435.

Printed in the United States.

Cover Photo credit: Peter Arnold, Inc.
Interior Photo credits: Peter Arnold, Inc.

Edited by Bob Italia

Library of Congress Cataloging-in-Publication Data

Prevost, John F.
  Sperm whales/ by John F. Prevost.
    p. cm. — (Whales)
Includes bibliographical references (p.23) and Index.
ISBN 1-56239-478-9
1. Sperm whale—Juvenile literature. [1. Sperm whale. 2. Whales.] I. Title.
II. Series: Prevost, John F. Whales.
QL737.C435P74   1995
599.5'3—dc20   95-12364
                                                   CIP
                                                    AC

ABOUT THE AUTHOR
John Prevost is a marine biologist and diver who has been active in conservation and education issues for the past 18 years. Currently he is living inland and remains actively involved in freshwater and marine husbandry, conservation and education projects.

Contents

SPERM WHALES AND FAMILY 4

SIZE, SHAPE AND COLOR 6

WHERE THEY LIVE 8

SENSES 10

DEFENSE 12

FOOD 14

BABIES 16

SPERM WHALE FACTS 18

GLOSSARY 20

INDEX 22

BIBLIOGRAPHY 23

SPERM WHALES AND FAMILY

Sperm whales are **mammals** that live in the sea. Like humans they are **warm-blooded**, breathe air with lungs, and **nurse** their young with milk.

Sperm whales are named for the **spermaceti organ** which fills most of their large head. Whalers still hunt sperm whales. But laws limit the numbers caught and protect some **breeding grounds**.

Sperm whales are the largest of the toothed whales. Sperm whales have two smaller relatives: the pygmy whale and dwarf sperm whale.

Sperm whales are the largest of the toothed whales.

SIZE, SHAPE
AND COLOR

The largest male sperm whales once were 62 feet (19 meters) long. But **whalers** took them all.

Males reach 54 to 59 feet (16.5 to 18 meters) in length. The females reach 37 to 43 feet (11.4 to 13.2 meters) in length.

A sperm whale has a large blocky head. Most of the head is filled with the **spermaceti organ**. Scientists believe this organ helps the whale when diving. It also helps it make loud sounds.

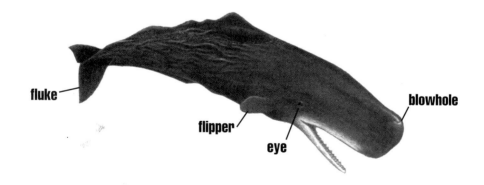

fluke

flipper

eye

blowhole

A male sperm whale can grow to 59 feet (18m).

Like all whales, the sperm whale breathes air through its **blowhole**. It is located at the front of the head and slightly left of center.

Sperm whales are dark gray in color. They are lighter on their undersides.

WHERE THEY LIVE

Sperm whales are found in oceans all over the world. They **migrate** from **polar** waters to **temperate** and **tropical** waters. They are found in the cooler waters during the summer. Males and females follow different migratory paths. They are often found in water deeper than 590 feet (180 meters).

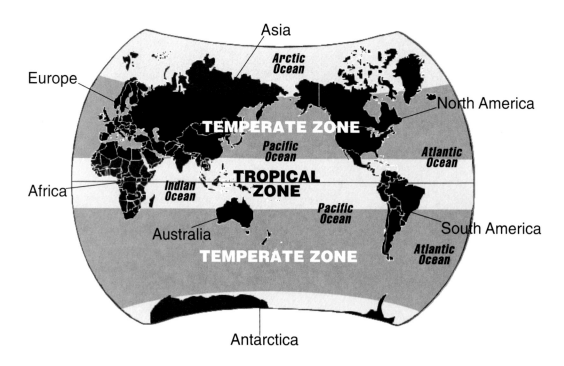

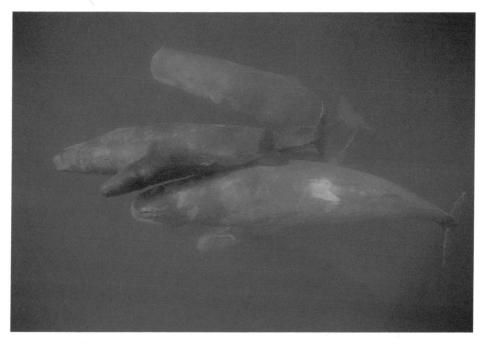

Sperm whales are social animals. They often travel in pods.

There are 5 different types of sperm whale **pods**: a **nursery** pod of females and calves, a **juvenile** pod, a **bachelor** pod of young males, a **bull** pod of **mature** males, and a mature female pod. There are 1 to 100 members in each pod.

SENSES

Sperm whales and people have 4 of the same senses. Their eyesight is good in and out of the water. If they wish to see above the water, they either bob their head above the surface or leap out of the water.

Hearing is an important sense. Water passes on sound better than air. That's because water is thicker than air and sound travels faster and farther in it.

Sperm whales make very loud clicks underwater. These clicks help them locate **prey** and talk to each other.

HOW ECHOLOCATION WORKS

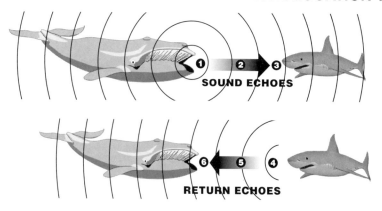

SOUND ECHOES

RETURN ECHOES

The whale sends out sound echoes (1). These echoes travel in all directions through the water (2). The sound echoes reach an object in the whale's path (3), then bounce off it (4). The return echoes travel through the water (5) and reach the whale (6). These echoes let the whale know where the object is, how large it is, and how fast it is moving.

A scientist working with a baby sperm whale.

Sperm whales listen to echoes returning from their clicks and can "see" around them. This is called **echolocation**. Scientists believe the **spermaceti** helps increase the clicking sound.

Touch and taste are also well-developed senses. Sperm whales do not have a sense of smell.

DEFENSE

Because of their size and strength, adult sperm whales have no known enemies other than man. Early whaling records show that sperm whale hunting was also very dangerous for the whalers. The large sperm whales crushed small wooden boats. The danger to the whaler ended when the **harpoon** cannon and giant whaling ships were used.

Sperm whales were hunted for the **spermaceti organ's** waxy oil. This oil was used in lamps and candles. Sperm whales were also hunted for **ambergris**, a hard lumpy substance found in the end of each sperm whale's **intestine**. Ambergris is used in perfumes.

Sperm whales are still hunted for spermaceti oil, ambergris and their meat. Laws now limit sperm whale hunting.

Sperm whales were hunted for the spermaceti organ's waxy oil and ambergris, a substance used to make perfume.

FOOD

Sperm whales eat **squid**, octopus, and fish. These whales can dive at least 6,500 feet (2,000 meters) deep. During deep dives, the whales may hold their breath up to one hour.

Scientists believe that the **spermaceti** helps sperm whales dive. The whales can change the thickness of the spermaceti. This helps the whales sink faster during a dive, or rise faster when returning to the surface. The spermaceti may also help the whales hunt for food.

Like other toothed whales, sperm whales hunt with **echolocation**. Some scientists believe sperm whales may stun **prey** with loud clicks. The spermaceti's shape helps sperm whales make a very loud noise.

This deep-sea octopus is a favorite food of the sperm whale.

BABIES

A baby sperm whale is called a **calf**. A calf is born 13 feet (4 meters) long. The calf **nurses** for up to 42 months. After it is **weaned,** the calf needs its mother and **pod** for food, safety, and **social** life.

A female sperm whale does not become an adult until it is 7 to 12 years old. A male becomes an adult when it is 18 to 19 years old.

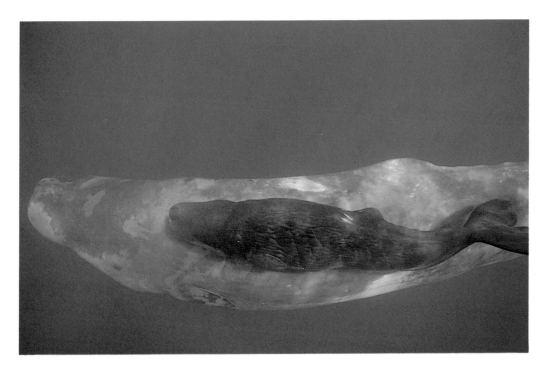

A sperm whale mother and calf in the Atlantic Ocean. Their skin peels when they rub against each other.

SPERM WHALE FACTS

Scientific Name: *Physeter macrocephalus*

Average Size:

54 to 59 feet (16.5 to 18 meters) - males

37 to 43 feet (11.4 to 13.2 meters) - females

62 feet (19 meters) - largest measured, a male

Where They're Found:

In all oceans. They prefer deep water, and avoid ice packs in **polar** seas.

A young sperm whale.

GLOSSARY

AMBERGRIS (AM-ber-gris) - A product of the sperm whale's intestine used in perfume, also called gray amber.

BACHELOR (BATCH-lor) - A male animal that has not taken a mate.

BLOWHOLE - A nostril (or nostrils) found on the top of the whale's head.

BREEDING GROUNDS - A territory where young are produced.

BULL - A male whale.

CALF - A baby whale.

ECHOLOCATION (ek-oh-low-KAY-shun) - The use of sound waves to find objects.

HARPOON - A heavy barbed spear used to kill whales and other large sea animals.

INTESTINE - The lower part of an animal's digestive tract.

JUVENILE - Young or youthful.

MAMMAL - A class of animals, including humans, that have hair and feed their young milk.

MATURE - Fully grown and able to reproduce.

MIGRATION (my-GRAY-shun) - To travel periodically from one region to another in search of food or to reproduce.

NURSE - To feed a young animal or child milk from the mother's breasts.

NURSERY - Area where young receive care.

ORGAN - A part of an animal that has a specific function.

POD - A group of a similar kind or type.

POLAR - Either the Arctic (north pole) or Antarctic (south pole) regions.

PREY - Animals that are eaten by other animals.

SOCIAL - Living in organized groups.

SPERMACETI (spur-muh-SET-ee) - A wax obtained from the head of a sperm whale; also the organ filling most of the head of a sperm whale.

SQUID - Sea animals related to the octopus that are streamlined in shape and have at least ten arms.

TEMPERATE (TEM-prit) - The part of the Earth where the oceans are not very hot, or not very cold.

TROPICAL (TROP-ih-kul) - The part of the Earth near the equator where the oceans are very warm.

WARM-BLOODED - An animal whose body temperature remains the same and warmer than the outside air or water temperature.

WEANED - To make a child or young animal used to food other than the mother's milk.

Index

A

air 10
ambergris 12

B

babies 16
bachelor pod 9
blowhole 7
breeding grounds 4
bull pod 9

C

calf 9, 16
candles 12
color 7

D

defense 12
diving 6, 14
dwarf 4

E

echoes 11
echolocation 10, 11, 14
enemies 12
eyesight 10

F

female pod 9
fish 14
food 14

H

harpoon 12
head 4, 6, 7
hearing 10
humans 4, 12
hunting 4, 12, 14
hunting laws 4, 12

I

intestine 12

J

juvenile pod 9

L

lamps 12
lungs 4

M

mammals 4
migration 8
milk 4

N

nurse 4, 16
nursery pod 9

O

oceans 8, 18
octopus 14
oil 12

P

perfumes 12
pod 9, 16
polar waters 8, 18

prey 10, 14
pygmy 4

S

sea 4, 18
senses 10, 11
shape 6
size 6, 18
smell 11
social life 16
sound 6, 10, 11, 14
sperm whale facts 18
sperm whale, female
  6, 8, 16
sperm whale, male
  6, 8, 16
spermaceti
  4, 6, 11, 12, 14
squid 14
summer 8

T

taste 11
temperate waters 8
toothed whales 4
touch 11
tropical waters 8

W

warm-blooded 4
water 10
weaning 16
whalers 4, 12
whaling 12
whaling ships 12

BIBLIOGRAPHY

Cousteau, Jacques-Yves. *The Whale, Mighty Monarch of the Sea*. N.Y.: Doubleday, 1972.

Dozier, Thomas A. *Whales and other Sea Mammals*. Time-Life Films, 1977.

Leatherwood, Stephen. *The Sierra Club Handhook of Whales and Dolphins*. San Francisco, Califonia: Sierra Club Books, 1983.

Minasian, Stanley M. *The World's Whales*. Washington, D.C.: Smithsonian Books, 1984.

Ridgway, Sam H., ed. *Mammals of the Sea*. Springfield, Illinois: Charles C. Thomas Publisher, 1972.

DATE DUE

MAY 5 '98			
MAY 26 '98			
MAY 17 '99			
OCT 07 '99			
MAY 24 02			
MAY 30 03			
MAY 20 04			
APR 19			
MAR 08 06			
FEB 17 07			
JAN 22			

The Library Store #47-0102